salmonpoetry

Fold of the Map
Joseph P. Wood

Published in 2014 by
Salmon Poetry
Cliffs of Moher, County Clare, Ireland
Website: www.salmonpoetry.com
Email: info@salmonpoetry.com

Copyright © Joseph P. Wood, 2014

ISBN 978-1-908836-72-4

All rights reserved. No part of this publication may be reproduced or transmitted in any form or by any means, electronic or mechanical, including photography, recording, or any information storage or retrieval system, without permission in writing from the publisher. The book is sold subject to the condition that it shall not, by way of trade or otherwise, be lent, resold or otherwise circulated without the publisher's prior consent in any form of binding or cover other than that in which it is published and without a similar condition, including this condition, being imposed on the subsequent purchaser.

COVER PHOTOGRAPHY: *Jessie Lendennie*
COVER DESIGN & TYPESETTING: *Siobhán Hutson*
Printed in Ireland by Sprint Print

Acknowledgments

I wish to thank the editors of the following magazines where some of these poems first appeared or are scheduled to appear, sometimes in a very different version and/or with a different title:

42opus: "Pensacola Beach, March"
Boston Review: "Anniversary," "The Spot"
Barnwood: "Jesus Christ, Your Uterus"
Backwards City Review: "After Whitman"
Copper Nickel: "First Sobriety"
ditch: Selections from "Tuskegee National Forest Suite"
Drunken Boat: "Mobile Bay, Late April"
elimae: Selection from "Tuskegee National Forest Suite"
Front Porch: "A Slender Epoch"
Natural Bridge: "After Baika"
New Delta Review: Selection from "Tuskegee National Forest Suite"
Oranges & Sardines: "Biography" and "Functions of Son"
Otoliths: Selections from "Tuskegee National Forest Suite"
Passages North: "Entering Vegas from the East, Wee Hours"
The Pedestal Magazine: Selections from "Tuskegee National Forest Suite"
Poetry London: "Delta Bound" (Originally as "Inside/Outside")
Sawbuck: "Confession to the Cuyahoga"
Typo: "Anatomy of a Bullet Wound"
Venereal Kittens: Selection from "Tuskegee National Forest Suite"
Zone 3: "A History"

Some of these poems also appear in the chapbook *Travel Writing*, Scantily Clad Press (2009).

"Urgency" also appears as a special edition mini-chapbook of the same name, *Cannibal Books* (2010).

Contents

I.

Autobiography	11
Delta Bound	12
Anatomy of a Bullet Wound	16
Functions of Son	17
A History	18
Dreams of the Bullied	20
The Medievalist	21
Urgency	22

II.

The Spot	29
The Milquetoast	31
In Our Fair City	32
A Slender Epoch	33
Snuff	34
First Sobriety	35
Confession to the Cuyahoga	36
Mobile Bay, Late April	37
Entering Vegas from the East, Wee Hours	38
From a Ward	39

III.

Carpetbagging: Tuskegee National Forest Suite   43

IV.

After Baika	57
Travel Writing	58
Anniversary	59
Jesus Christ, Your Uterus	61
Oakland, I Think	62
Puget Sound, May	63
Pensacola Beach, March	64
Frog & Toad Aren't Friends	65
After Whitman	66
I Could Say	67

I.

AUTOBIOGRAPHY

grand as Lagos mine
disaster, cruel like Beijing
prison cells, starts & stutters
in my father's unshaven
ghost, his one night white
Russian, slurred sentiment
upon hearing Brady caught
Reagan's bullet, *son, the stars
are pointless, ditto the planets,*
I turned for my mother but
she was the street, the dive-
bombing snow, El' hurdling
darkness I wished to sip,
narcotic snore, greyhound-
like twitching, in my dream
I became my dream
electrified with a bugle, soldiers'
hard-ons flown half-mast,
thesauruses where Purple
Hearts were pinned, it's a lie
to claim there are 30 words
for glory, 28 which I know
will never cross my lips
when the funeral car
stops, the sun daggers
its burn, the dead man's
collar like a dog-eared page
I did not fold nor write.

DELTA BOUND

For Nathan

Remember the trash bag hanging out the busted window
of the rusted-through corrugated trailer & you said
that ain't no bag, that, dumbass, is a small girl's hand, she
smiled a mouth full of water moccasins & one had fallen out
to the swamp where her mama stood ankle-deep beating it
with a hoe & the road dipped down past the bleached
sycamores & the ball fields had river grass dried & ravaged &
the Frisbee golf buckets were painted a bright green

& you were asking me about why my mother had a face
time chose to unhinge like bad gears in a pick-up truck
hell took out to the backwoods to let die only the squirrels
turned into a city, with deep pockets of acorns & dried
dung clinging to cracked, leather interior, & remember you
said, drive big boy, & we backed up down the dock's wood
splintering beneath the wheels & we fell into the mighty

Mississippi & got carried down to a sand barge & waved
to everyone man we thought might be Twain, & you said I
know he's as alive as that last flame in that last mind fading
in Nagasaki, & you said I should've been there with you
inside Fat Man's shell & saw the grid-like patterns
the earth makes to fool you to thinking nothing alive
in its beige, abstract strips where slash pines might or
might not flourish, nothing bad never happens except

women rub charcoal into their half-starved babies' eyes
so they don't see their fathers leaning against the brick
wall of the overly-graffitied rural-town project, he & friends
laughing & coughing, some swollen with gout, others
fiddling with absurdly loose diabetic socks, & one of them
will lose a foot, its tissue green & lined with urine salt,
& another man will blow his own face out with a twelve
gauge & be that story everyone tells, no one believes,

remember when my teenage, mental-case friend with benefits
decided to evacuate her skull of its cerebral jewels
& left me a note, & blamed me for every little innocuous
semen drop I left on her belly when I stood up, shook
myself off, & stepped into the bathroom & heard
the neighbors yell about that roofing business that lost
its license, & you said she never said come back here
baby, but she said it all right, & I have the knickknacks

to prove it, the Czech throwaway plates her mother
bought on the side of the road as the Russians
raised their AK's & the next thing she knew she awoke
on a commercial plane skidding its way to Heathrow
& remember when I told you her mother always disapproved
of the British culinary tradition of taking perfectly good
offal & blanching into inedible mush, what they needed
was a good stone soup, a spice rack of floor sweepings

where one minute a roach skittered away from the crack
of daylight the health inspector shed onto the kitchen
unsealing it like a tomb, the next minute the roach drew
long hard breaths, shot up through its shell, bipedal,
human-born, & talking & talking & talking about the slow
talk of dumb people who never knew nothing about
any damn thing concerning fishing, all the while you made

love to a woman next to a gar-fish's rotting carcass
whose nose you used to play the musical saw, remember
you felt the fine, blond hairs on your neck ingrown hearing
that instrument's spooky melody, all the world wanted
you said sometimes was a high hat & snare drum
given to a meth-addict, we laughed, you passed the bong
we bought from those hippies on the Quebec border

no one can sneak across anymore, though everything
still comes back shrouded in nimbus emptied of rain,
so many lovers lost inside a fog, a massive barrel
making decent a nudist colony of fat men, & I touch
the big schnoz my nose once was until that girl's lumber-
jack father punched it clear across my swollen, blue cheek,
the weeping & the wheezing, the anvils that were my legs

& the winter lightning which was God, & you said, dude,
that island ain't an island, that's a time machine where
Elizabethans have hidden themselves from the Jamestown
colony & ordered one another to buttfuck & sure as shit
their eyes smelled of poverty, they lived sans toilets & their
wells were done bone dry, & still they opened their doors,
touched me lightly on the shoulders, called me son,

& nothing bad happened for many, many nights, only
the little nubs of stars burning lightly but insistently down
beneath the cypress saplings some genius brought
from California, & remember how he sautéed such delicate
cod cheeks, his toddler daughter insisted on using a potty
whose former life was a lobster pot, & everyone kept laughing

until I asked, why do you stay in a strip of shoreline
where the Martians shine their intrusive strobe lights on
& they said, kids need roots, & I laughed, asshole
clenched tight, their glares cutting like chicken marinated
in laxatives, do you remember how I drank that night,
sure they were nice people with nice hardwood floors

stretching out toward the forest, which forest, I can't say
that I remember each twisted branch, how they twined
around themselves like swollen arthritic hands, & remember
you said, son, that's the story of the earth, & remember
you said I once said, this ain't the earth & I ain't your son
but of course, I turned from the mop closet functioning
as my bedroom, & I pulled back the covers when you left
& yanked my meat to pictures of women kissing themselves

14

in mirrors, & you once barged in, put a train
ticket in my hand, land slowly sliding from delta to mountain,
Loblolly to Saguaro, & I saw snow for the last
time when I was ten, remember, you were my friend
who kept pushing me into the side of the batting cage
& I threw my helmet, & I ripped off my batting gloves,
& the mound was a diamond, & the diamond knew my name.

ANATOMY OF A BULLET WOUND

Zipped inside an evidence bag, a wrist
    watch insists there's a future
        of snow-packed fields, empty
            coats, trampled casings.

The open, upturned eye promises
    so much stagnant, black water
        & the hole where the other eye would be
            a thin blood crust.

Tape recorders & one word headlines
    will crumble to dust. Thought bubbles
        bloat the family: the gun from behind,
            no perpendicular, was there a knife

left on the sill, & his rock-nicked window,
    the bed unmade, sheets in clumps,
        & what was the name
            on that framed baseball card?

House lights snap on. Blink off.
    So goes the street, monument to vespers
        of fizzling phone line, hanging sneakers
            encased in frost

like mastodons, who bowed to drink,
    lifted to yelp—The river reeds trembled.
        The current slowed. Nimbus sunk
            & spread the valley,

which forked & fractured, God's weak foot.

FUNCTIONS OF SON

I was your rope bridge. I was your chasm. I the eyes my siblings magpied. I the optic scraps. The unfurled copper wire. The falling beams, the gutted house. Was the shoebox of yard. The brown, brown Augustine grass. The pollen fleets, the kudzu clinging. And cling I did. Implode I did. Stomped my larynx, offered it catlike. I philandered, I rumored. I undermined neighbors. Declawed their infants, chicken poxed cats. I sandbagged the snow. I brought you the Styx. Called it a spring, freshened your highball. You were a thick thread of droll. A brain verging collapse. Three day stubble, a mealy-mouthed suitcase. There was a bus. Let us be that bus. I'll lead you by hand. I'll call you sweet duckling.

A HISTORY

Speeding to your father's gravesite,
Lil' sis punched me in the arm. I shoved

back & she kicked & hair pulled clumps
& you should rip out our fucking eyes

& let them dangle, that's what you said
maybe. I slumped the frayed seats

bursting yellow stuffing, & smacked
gum. Acid bloomed my gut: That feeling

where a bright light flashes, skin melts,
each regret anvils out the mouth

& that becomes one's life. Remember
you said to have a son was to get

your arm caught in a wood chipper? Maybe
we were driving to euthanize the cat.

She shredded & pissed the kitchen carpet
so you laid down cheap, hexagonal tile

but the floor got wet & eventually caved.
In those holes lay darker, wetter holes

where I was born. Remember those
glue traps? How the mice would gnaw

their own legs off & drag their masticated
selves into the wall. Maybe they became

one vast, dark heaven. Here's a prayer:
your mother's offer to raise me—garbled,

stuttered, Avalanche of Apology you couldn't
drive fast enough. You hammered the horn

& snaked the lanes & the oil pan
dropped so we stopped. You scrutinized:

The horizon a large jigsaw, the clouds
a sheet over furniture. Was I sixteen

& Lil' sis an unmitigated disaster
razoring each arm & pulling out muscle

like bright red knots? Don't the Chinese
write down their wishes & tie them

with a bow? And send them downstream?
Water has so much responsibility. Not like me,

that's what you said. And so much more
fire shot down your back. Your discs had crumbled.

The doctors could do nothing. You smoked
in the dim room & drank Diet Coke for supper.

The television showed missing girls in wells
& stadiums imploding. Remember the Phillies?

They stunk for like a decade. We'd listen
to Harry Kalas get sloshed on the air.

Their closer couldn't find a baseball
in a baseball factory. That's what you said.

DREAMS OF THE BULLIED

For my birthday, I will receive no face-deep, double-chocolate swirly in the toilet. And I certainly won't cede my non-existent lunch money for a good swift liver shot. I'll march over to Kim Conte, her welfare cheese sandwich, her squadron of head lice, & enlist her. Ditto Steven Lamont, Michael Jacquinto, Emily "Nasal Drip" Drobile, every bottlenoser & overbitten pipsqueak. We'll unfurl of our white flags & urinate on them. We'll razorblade the douchbagged & use their heads for soccer balls. Our teachers always said *the world should not just happen to you, be a verb!* But our teachers smelled like chalk & drove sad, dented compacts & had marriages that had dwindled to sputters of smoke. Through a blackened eye, I watched them scroll the same damn formula each day on the board, as if they'd never learn, this was the day I'd coldcock a falconer, steal his black glove, & feel flight reverberate my hand, those small, gelatin knuckles.

THE MEDIEVALIST

At the point of a gaggle, after we beat through the sumac & brambles, in the alley I stood akimbo, head slightly tilted, like a quotient or a riddle, what could I say?

Yes, that was a cat crucified on plywood. Yes, that was its heart publicly beating above long, hard wheezing, & Tommy Giraudi, behind us crouching down, nail gun in the left hand, & tightly smiling.

No one puked. No one launched or laughed. We entered the grade school a little later the next day, shifty & fidgeting, unable to stare at our books

cause we were staring down the side of a volcanic cliff: one side was dry & littered with medium-security penitentiaries; the other small animals were subsumed in lava.

I can't tell you what became of my friends. What becomes of anything that clutters the earth? All I know

is the farm lands started to wither, & the snow peaks in the background chanted like schizophrenic monks. Then the gnats swelled to the size of bibles, & when they bit, I wouldn't swear.

URGENCY

birthed
from the snowcap
bowl, bowels,
night, metaphor
for night, dawn
papa went
for a glass of
milk, pulled out
a shotgun, Braille

        of agony, O, O, O
my hands are scissors,
incisors, I'm piecing
back his brain, pirating
a clipper ship, navigating
the Cape of

Good Hope,
    kelp shores,
        electromagnetic sand,
            bipedal starfish, with
blue eyes, baby puke, lolling tongues,
blue mouth, the baby's eyes, I'm in the crib, I am the crib,
        O, O, O
like mama & her dark moods, like a room one enters & the room falls
like a snow of glass, a shard of rain, now black, now gray, & graying
        O, O, O

Here is a hammer, here is a radio
Here is a voice, here that voice
gagged, a gaggle, geese

                waddle in unison, their eye
                -ing bread
                      in my palm,

I am a palm, I am a bread, an oven
backfiring, Plath retracting
her neck from the gas, the gas from the air, the lung from the body,
    the body from the brain, there is a lake, there is a brain-pan,
    there is a tree pan, an elm hole, a worm kiss, small one,
    big one, brain, O, brain,
        tongue, O , tongue, never
        again, never
        again, & nor, & O, & O & heart, black
            & yellow,

& on & on, what is
the source, always backwards, what is
the source, always backwards
            swath of bones
elephant cry, pick up trunks,
do a little dance, that was
their baby, their pachyderm
Springtime, the violets
turn to posies, the plague comes
down again,

                then it is August
                & then the rainfall does
                fall, the levees
                do rupture
                or dynamite, citizens
                not citizens, no
                swollen, bloated feed-
                jackpot for mosquitoes,

        cameras pan left,
      rooftops submerged,
    the future
dead on said rooftops
save one or two
hundred, the helicopters

circle & circle & circle
whoosh whoosh whoosh down
                         the MC Escher
                         staircase, bookcase,
                         the bible on page one
                         sounds like page one
                         thousand like a thousand
                         drunk bees, like their hives
               exploding confetti, stingers
    inside wheelbarrows so much
depends upon who
barrows out to the rock shelf
collecting snow, an ox corpse
rotting, an eel falling
from the ox's mouth, snow collecting

on the village below, the rock shelf
above, its shivering snipers asleep, asleep,
here are their wives, disrobing, wet, lathered, pulling
their hair, then scalp, then skull, then brain mass, then ooze, count
                                         backwards
                                         from a million
                                         BC, pterodactyls
                                         flower out
                                         the pictures of
                                         pterodactyls in
                                         the textbook, circa

Ye Ole' Bearded One standing
on the Western Shoreline, chanting
                         future, future, future, O, O, O
                         the Inuit in the North, O, O, O
                         the Amazonian the South, O, O, O
                         the Alpian, the Himalayan,
                         Kilimanjaro, Andes, Andes, Andes

Bearded one, prognosticator, future

name of Philadelphian bridge
& the Soup factory on the left side
& the DOW chemical factory on the right side
& below the bridge, slow, brown river
where the tug boats go tug, tug
where the freighters go gurgle, gurgle
large metallic babies,
                    looking for their mothers,

dumb, dumb ships, every shore-
line is mother
& father, refuge
& refugee, & pen, & mouth,
& syllable,
& heart,
& God, of course
& God, of course, retread my face

Great New World, your ribs
the silt on the brown, slow river
next to the asylum abutting the village
& the snipers are still snipers
older & slower, a little more thoughtful:

when the bullet shatters bone
the planet sheds its ice.

II.

THE SPOT

Like a scar across the earth,
Like my fingers were peasants,

I touch where the penknife had
Plunged & stood. I watch you

Watch an oil tanker, its port-
Side scrawled in wide, fat lettering

I'd mistake for hieroglyphics
If not for your soft *I can read that*

Punctuated by a long, hard sigh.
Your neck's scent conjures ore-

Rich dirt, stands of date trees
As far as my eye can't fathom but

In spades, they shaded our porch,
Lined our colonnade even when—

You throw a pebble at nothing
You'd want to haul to the next life

After this next life: this chemical plant
We've trespassed, we're boozed.

Stories pour forth & I hear
Zilch, just imagine you shrieking

As if you found where hell came
To die, & now you bear its etching

On your fleshy bulb of knee
My hand keeps brushing. Dawn's

Past. You want eggs. From
A booth we scrutinize passers-by:

This one caustic, this soul-shattered,
Most just bored with their lives.

The sun is full through the window.
I don't recall your last name.

THE MILQUETOAST

Love is pedagogical. Don't buy drinks for women who work in a knife factory. Don't say her hair is luminous & could house a family of owls. Go about your business, eyeing the ice in your cup, pretending the cubes are great boats. Dream of a country absent acid-reflux. Scribble a speech about tunnels of light that can eviscerate your face. Voilà, you've mutated: a judge who offers succinct opinions upon request, a president who winks in the mirror and the glass winks back. Behind every good man is his smack-addicted doppelganger. Love is that addict's match. Love is that bent, burnt spoon.

IN OUR FAIR CITY

I once saw a knife go through a man

as if the dude wasn't there, & I suppose he wasn't

once the blade, dripping thinly, dotting the train floor, was released

& something birdlike went up up to the tenement-ed skyline,

then we tunneled under the city & the car stopped.

Everyone was screaming. The knife, in fact, was a teenage girl

who dropped & crumbled to a fine powder the transit cops

scooped up with their hands. Another El' came to fish us,

& thank God, we said, weren't we lucky, we said, we have work

but work had us by the scruff of the neck, took us up to daylight

where taxicabs napped & pretzel vendors went belly-up.

That girl, now a girl again, stood at a blinking traffic light, waved

for me to join her—like an old friend. She grabbed my hand,

waltzed me to a deep hug, sprouted wings, grew a grasshopper head.

You are a blade of grass, she said. Then her insect mouth opened.

A SLENDER EPOCH

Under the El', where storefronts are chained
& every other building graffiti, they have a name,
"Tai-Wal hookers", a cleaning agent, inhaled—
The brain goes to mush. *Tai Wal* transforms

to *Thailand*: O the honeymoons, the surf,
save those skyscraper waves, fishing boat
flotsam, wing-snapped gulls, a woosh…
Flood recedes: wish it hadn't: bloated tourist

passports float the South Pacific. The salt,
day by day, bleaches the face, erases
pinpoint eyes, & say you found, on gutted
shoreline, this strange negative space, a name

without an owner. The sunset goes
metallic. Someone's scrawled an epithet
in the sand, whose syllables sound
like flies, the underworld's flaring.

SNUFF

On the screen, a woman fed so many pain pills she could've just been a mop. My friends—good friends—had pulled out beer bongs, bowls of potato chips, & hollowed-out apples to use as hash pipes. Then someone pulled a gun—a middle-aged dude with a head-scar zigzagging from pate to nose—& shot the woman in front of the camera. A bomb went off

in my chest, & I scanned the room like the edges of the earth & saw nothing. I left. One minute, the sky was a conflagration of dying stars, the next, the sun flashed orange & a seagull pecked my ear as I slept on a dock. Waking, I never felt so—

FIRST SOBRIETY

I'd like to say I pondered
a dusk, fire threatening to eat stars.
With an exaggerated wave, I turned

my gaze—brown & flotsam
waterfall, dam stress-fractured here
& there—& gained seismic introspection.

It didn't work that way. I
mule-kicked the phone. The broom
swept my last friends, & was closeted.

I came to fidget a rhinestone lighter
each morning, slump the kitchen table,
& stare into its faint blue flame

like a monk befuddled by the moon.
And say he teetered from precipitous bluff,
owls' clipped cries as rain turned mist,

yes, they still existed: each apology
I never could articulate, each mistake
I wished would fall like eye-sand, yes,

this is where I lived those days—
where the dirt turned rust, where rust
encased the pines, & no one told me

my mouth would erode. One by one
regrets came forward like unknown
offspring, & having no backbone, I left.

CONFESSION TO THE CUYAHOGA

I'd unclench a drowning man's arm.
I'd covet a yacht's morose anchors.

River which crests the sandbags, which makes the lake homes
Memories of lake homes, I am but a tool

                                            Forgive me. Forgive

My socks, unrolled, moth-chewed. Forgive
My feet, unwashed, propped atop my backpack.

If every dockside smokestack is a chute to the underworld
Then every smokestack's brick is a choice:
                                      To spit once
Or to spit twice, or to simply paper-bag my vodka.

Daylight savings dusk has ceased
And the oil in the water & the water shouldn't be the same—

Floating, crushed milk jug   you are my catamaran.

MOBILE BAY, LATE APRIL

God, my patience is thinning
Out across the bay
                     & the trawling fisherman,
Their barren hooks & thick crowfeet say
Cancer can't be worse than this
Potholed causeway
                     Jutting & expanding
Over ocean, toward the nimbus …

The cruise ships are delusional.
Magnolia-grooved mansions

Wind the other direction, past the Navy's
Metallic graveyard & 24/7 bail bond
Shop whose neon blinks
                     The future. I touch
A rabid squirrel's tail
Cause it lets me. In the square
A bum slumps his shopping cart, his bric-a-brac

An extension of his face. Each swollen eyelid
An island. God, You sail
His diseased cornea. It does not hurt
Him: cirrhosis throes, eternal.

ENTERING VEGAS FROM THE EAST, WEE HOURS

No, the valley's on fire. No, the stars have landed & are bulky, desert shrubs. No, heaven's been dumped here. No, my mistake, it's next to the hotel key, left backside pocket. No, I plan to avoid irrational exuberance. No, I plan to feast on surf, turf, & imp's blood. No, I left my pity with the street boys. No, their eyelashes stretch to the Colorado. No, the river is full of money. No, the river is a vast swirling sound. No, that pyramid of light is not a suggestion. No, the party dresses are not filled with people. No, I lost the cocaine. No, I lost the address. No, it's a quiet space, filled with well-coifed Buddhists. No, please don't circumnavigate the strip clubs. No, please don't zip us to the suburbs. No, those can't be the gauche nouveau mansions. No, the entire cul-de-sac's foreclosed. No, that's a gauntlet of wind. No, that's a scurrying mouse. No, that's a swooping owl.

FROM A WARD

The rain does what it does 300 days a year here, sky so gray it's boring as that letter I sent last decade—one immense diatribe against a woman whose flaw existed in her hands—their inability to usher my hourly malaise to a cartoon hole, perpetual tumbling.

Now I get it. Why kelp piles up like debt. Why the shore insists on more. A lunatic would call this beauty, but that lunatic boarded the eve's last ferry. Thus remains the fog, an inscrutable quotient.

In a different universe, there are sunspots—great red flares stuttering across the cosmos. Nothing lives, nothing dies, & that seems a good thing—It's not: No variations in the stratosphere. One emotion, one voice. The greatest star I know a light-shot toddler.

III.

CARPETBAGGING: TUSKEGEE NATIONAL FOREST SUITE

~

Among the Loblollies & splattered toads, kudzu
wraps metal rusted gates, black flies little clouds
above each headstone, names the names of paper-
mills yielded, decades ago, to swamps & light
-ning, armadillo shit & four wheel exhaust—
for each letter in a name, a petal dropped
from rose bushes on the neatly mowed field's
far left quadrant, the wind so unlike a wail.

::

Born I of the stars, masquerading as shards
of glass, my name is Sad-Ear-Glued-to-Phone,
my mother the ocean lost inside
her own womb. Such sad chords
sings the sparrow glued to the Monkey Bar
outside the Sonny Hill Recreation Center, North Philly USA
if the USA a drained swimming pool, its citizens
boas left in a box, writhing.

~

A falling

shack, roof blown

clear beyond sight. Still

inside someone coughs, spits

tobacco, the memory of

crunch crunch crunch dried leaves

like snow drifting about the parlor.

On the fireplace lies a shotgun.

In the muzzle half-decayed squirrel.

∵

What if I fired a bullet

& the Milky Way were a vacuum

& no bird interrupted its flight

& humans were simple, bland

quarks with no hands?

Parabola path

& out blows my skull's back: a thousand

basketballs erupt, two thousand pick-up teams

behind—small children following, their children next...

~

Cold's what
I'd say
if snow
could be
born here—

::

Every part of my father's brain archipelago
against the wall: how very Indonesian—

Sometimes the plane misses my signal fire;
Sometimes the coconut phone shorts out;

Duh, I'm in a city dense as obtuse-
ness itself, people lost among the choir of rickshaws

though I've commandeered a taxi, though the driver stops
for evening prayers, though I mis-mouth blessings

I mean them. That's how it was to love
that massive volcano: molten, molten, molten

no hint of ash, ever.

~

Neo-Gothic church, fix me: so utterly cliché
my peek through the newly sawed door's slight

crack at snake handlers inside—gawking now
& guffawing at strummed Amazing Grace on banjo.

So utterly cliché to imagine the fifteen people—
washed-out girl in washed-out pinafore, father

in tie too small, sister sucking back a liter
of snot—spilling out into the noonlight, driving off

in rickety pickups. So utterly cliché to slump
beneath the bare black cherry trees, & shake

like God himself is turning back my eyelid.
Behind the steeple's dried well, my Doppelganger

emerges, punches my face clear onto the rocks.

::

>Why make each day a hemorrhage,
>& why equate breathing with moving
>
>the lake from the basin? No one loves
>
>a self-made corpse. Violence taught me
>to carry my own rope, & neurosis
>
>how to fret about the slipknot. Live or die,
>
>the slow alphabet of streetlights
>articulating that woman's shock of dyed red
>
>hair bouncing to her own long strut
>as if she owned an earth
>
>that would make me whole.

~ :: ~

The rifle boom means
        something's alive & something,

if the aim is true, won't be: My Darling,

there's a place in your mind, you say,

an onyx lake   with hard, clean air

      & if I went there,   tar would geyser
                                                  & your brain would

fossilize…   now something screeches

& your robe flies open—owls

                rupture your hymen
                                        & milk waterfalls your

chest, those two foothills where
                                          a deer draws
                                  its last breath, you say,

            going there.

~

South Sandy Road connects the real world, State 82, to

Three hogs, hail-pelted on their snouts, puddle rolling

At the bottom of the hill, where dirt turns to slop, & slop to

Stuck, the Corolla, which has no business in the Big Boy World

Of 4 wheelers & Pabst Blue Ribbon, of *Hey What We Got Here* to *Humph*

And wouldn't you know, I should've kept my mouth shut, & shit

The three guys, packed tight among the dogs in the pick-up bed,

Hop out: one throws the car in neutral, other two pushing, me

Standing beside the dogs, car going back, back, back to

The real world where hail turns to rain, rain to fogged-up night.

::

> In a dream where the West Coast collapses, except for this one thin board of continental shelf, the shelf & I detach, hurl through space, & land above this fireplace in the Antebellum mansion slap-dab behind Piggly Wiggly, buy-one/get-one on pigs feet, pig cracklins, boiled eggs floating in a jar of pepper-fused vinegar, brought up from the Black Belt, alluvial plains of sweet potato & watermelons, a son

barefoot under the sun sinking deeper, deeper, the ringworm on his elbow, the belt cinched loosely around his scrawny waist, waste not want not, eat son eat, late afternoon, a different time now, sun is orange, tongue hanging gray, remember that dog, Lucy, she'd come up, eat the finger sandwiches off the porch, remember, that white bread, straight from the oven, & that dog's face, her sad slump, like she defecated in daddy's ash urn, that tongue, those brown drippy eyes, love me, & of course we did, my apparitional wife & I, her brown eyes like two forests in a white sea of foam, & I take my palm, & my lovely soul-mate spits in it, & we shake, & our son becomes two sons, & our love a pyramid of chopped firewood, & the night smells like night, all toads & raccoon crap, but that's how it should smell, that's what the dream says, the dream with the face, the face whose cheek tastes like the ocean when God himself removes the brine, & I am falling in the froth, & the froth goes up my nose, but I can breathe, & my love is there, husking stars like corn.

~

Coughing comes from random thickets or Winnebago in
    a clearing,
generator on its last legs, beer cans

everywhere. Fuck the census,
their lives do say: We'll lose our teeth on our damn dime.
They do

die of moccasin bites, can't read
the timber company's claim on
their land—they'll stand like soldiers

when the clear cut opens the light.

::

                Over the wide, hexagonal roofs
           of residence halls, where debutants

      walked arm-in-arm & football players
          spoke carefully, polysyllabically,

        my girlfriend turned to me & said
        I am not a dumpsite for your grief.

        It was like falling into a cravace,
      & hearing friends above wonder

         my whereabouts while I pulled
           a crampon out of my thigh.

~

The waxy leaves in this forest

The waxy leaves are like sheets

Of plastic encasing a couch

A couch at Grandma Nunziata-tina-nina, aka Nina

Dinners of angel hair, anchovies, bread crumbs, walnuts

A recipe scrawled on an index card yellowed & soup-stained

A card once her equally neurotic toy-collie, She-She, ingested

& rolled about the shoebox of yard, gut all clogged

Nina said sighing *you boy, go help your Nina's She-She*

The last thing she said before her eyes rolled back

Though trees, miraculously, shot up through the soil.

::

Broken, I start I-10 in that pit of stalled metal—LA—& ride, Mountain
 Dew-chased, twitchy, New Mexican desert long dull heat waves, car
  moves through El Paso, Stockton, Kerriville, then someone pours water
   in the sky-oven, the trees go canopy, & hundred thunk thunk
    miles, overpass above this endless swamp, & wait
     for something dark to enter, voodoo & all, no
      just flat city, canned jazz, & the Atlantic
       drifting somewhere South, now Biloxi,

dizzying sun, Mobile Bay, a battleship, Government Boulevard,
Springhill College, the sororities, the Friday night dance off
until their clothes come off, I lurking on the other side,
a beer in one hand, a cell phone in the other, you are
somewhere I think pouring alcohol, we talked maybe once
in ten months, & the time gap makes the moon look like steel
& the sorority sisters prodding aliens of light—wait, no, I remember
now, at the Unitarian Church contra dance, you hold a fiddle
which then becomes an accordion, & your face beats
the music into something that makes the elderly snap
to attention, & I wave to you, & you nod to me
& your black dress hangs at your shoulder
so sharply boned, a recrimination, a conversion
from no life to some life, a pull-out bed with bad springs
that you never say would be mine, but never say
it wouldn't, & I drink one more beer
that tastes like an eel, & the eel falls down my shirt
& I give birth to a hundred eels, & you hit them with hoe
which means you hit me with hoe, & I stutter back
& find you behind me, on bended knee, opened.

~::~

You say feel something
borderline gross
      like bologna in the dark
            covering a light

switch. I close my eyes. I tap my feet. My feet are boats

burdened by anchors.
      Lean your lips on this lobe
           My Love, kiss my

craniotomy. I see sand dunes. I see witchgrass. Newly minted

motels hurricaned.
      Come closer, love. Move on
             upstate, surrender

your lilt. To acres of nowhere. Summer's fat, mean mouth. Blow

harder, baby
      breeze, stir those black
           flies. Up I go

down to the swamp. Open your hand, My Love. What squalor.

~

What is the Bible Belt
when the snowbirds settle
& Boston-Brahmian-bred lawyers pontificate
& factories pop-open like azaleas of cement
& Quiceanera parades clog the major road's two arteries
& rib plates are served with kale & corn fused with salmon oil
& the former Walmarts, all Kafka-like, gain homemade Crescents
makeshift mosques, & bi-regional babies, father Good Old Boy, mother
from elsewhere, elsewhere, elsewhere, & will the children say Sir
& will the Ma'am abandon the Sun dress for the leather skirt
with the slit in the back as large as Olympus, why yes
where is the Savior, but on everyone's tongue
who noshes Schnitzel, German bakery,
order, order, order we ascribe to
the Germans, & their trains
run on time, especially
to here, & here.

::

Behind my rowhome
as a child George Washington
led his army over the biotite outcropping
on that very hill now overrun with raccoons
begging for the kids in rain-soaked alley below
to throw-up their bread scraps, but the kids are kids
playing games like overturn the tricycle, corner weak Jenny
& strip her jeans, Barney shirt, then run away, laughing
the kind of thing, I do believe, Washington fought
for.

IV.

AFTER BAIKA

Dumbfounded as I'd never been:
Newborn slimed in meconium.

The Space before her first cry
I charged like a quadruped. Still
The cherry trees bloomed too soon...

Snow fell: dandruff, confetti.
A nurse placed a mask on my wife's sweaty face.

The river had ice chunks.
The river had guppies.

A defibrillator was hauled from a corner.

And nothing broke the monks' chant.
And smoke spiraled the rock garden.
Fields shot everywhere. None were aflame.

TRAVEL WRITING

Avalanches of non-restrictive clauses, indeterminate subjects, & an ear you could set an oboe concerto to. *So as not to subjugate the other*, my friend would say & then he'd smoke his cigarette down to the nub before baseball batting whores who littered the streets of *Grand Theft Auto*. He spent nights shaking like a greyhound next to his wife, & his wife, tired of his restiveness, took up a with boxer ten years his junior. He was, to use the words of another friend, *a monstrous infant with insomnia*. And speaking of this other friend: he too passed the nights, alone, chronically drinking, & would often call my house stupefied, believing it was me who fled the rehab & decided to burn even larger holes in my liver. This decent human being, in a moment so drunk he could not help but utter honesty, blurted *Joe, you are by far the most ingratiating freak I have ever met*. And like that, I pulled myself from his life, as I pulled myself from the other writer's life when I grew weary of the same five dysfunctions leaking into every conversation—or so I told myself when I was staring into the mirror, once again, self-castigating. I forget what I did: it was so, so long ago. One of these friends is now dead & the other across the country with a new wife, a solid career, & by all accounts, a mellowness you can plop airplanes on. I, too, have morphed, but being me, I can't say how. I simply began this poem as one man & now am biking away, down the long dusty country road, toward the cattle, cottonwoods, & a river bisecting everywhere, even here, even here.

ANNIVERSARY

Possum skeleton crushed down
so deep into the road it's the road
where you found me, verge of sleeping
pill in my mouth chased with vodka
stored in my flask, & you got out of
that Nissan with the horrible timing
chain, touched my cheek in that careful
Midwestern way, I tossed the ripped
backpack which was my poor body
& we rode. Ice-laced rain broke
on the windshield only to re-atomize
in your wide, brown eyes measuring
the klutzy waltz I had with the vacuum
until I fell through your apartment's
cheap tile wall & into the meth addicts'
place next door: Flooded pantries,
flooded toilets, & clumps of hair
on their coffee table, you said baby
what we have here is what we might say
is a bad idea, like a drive thru liquor store
on Saturday night, like a tea-party
where the stuffed animals are decapitated
& the toddlers stand shell-shocked. You
waved your hand, a courtyard & small
bungalow flickered into being. You
opened the wrought iron gate, the ferns
went green upon your short lovely
fingers & you said I don't think we need
water. From there on out, your hair
undulated on the left side of your face
which smelled like chocolate bars
& lemon tree barks & never failed
to electrocute then defibrillate starlings.
You took off your shirt: diamonds wept.

You opened your mouth to kiss my
shoulder: every skeleton in every grave
erupted out of the ground clapping.
Why did you want me when I was
nothing like an Austen novel, nothing
worth putting an engine in, every word
I spoke like a turtle flipped on its shell,
its little legs kicking in that unintentionally
funny way turtles have of dying. You
knew we were bound to fall, the center
of a field of hay in rural Slovakia where
the villagers say, Fuck you, I love you,
& I know my hands are little claws
you slide rubber gloves on so I don't nip
& I worry you will see my face one day
& feel a disappointment turn granite
in your guts, but you were always an ace
with a chisel, a deep thinker in a seismic
era, & though I am broken in fifty ways
& though it's not your job to superglue
please again make me something other
than stuttering me: make me a baby.

JESUS CHRIST, YOUR UTERUS

feels like the entire Chinese diving team
    forced to triple pike again & again
        but the dives have such skittering
            panic, one assumes the team's

being threatened at gunpoint
    by the Red Army's best henchman
        who, for sadistic satisfaction, start
            blindfolding the athletes who

look nothing like athletes
    rather, like malnourished swallows
        wings clipped, feather plucked
            all the while outside clouds

start to hemorrhage question
    marks, & on the lake, the ducks
        tuck their faces beneath
            an obsidian-hued surface,

that, beyond comprehension,
    turns blacker the further it goes
        until the water hits a wall
            & on the wall's other side

is a bigger, thicker wall
    & all around, the muffled laughs
        of people, the clickety-clack
            of shoes, & there I am,

in a space you never dreamed, hanging.

OAKLAND, I THINK

In their faces, someone punches infants

& someone else snaps the photo, downloads

all across this great blue ball of disappointment

& across the dented streets refusal to apologize

for seducing the BB guns with its hot red octagon,

the color of Chlamydia, the shades of virulent snot

my friend Myron tries to wipe in fast circles

from the homeless, & he knows the street's just a pit

where sailboats deposit their cargo, captains' faces

slowly going to rust, & he told me where this pit

lies down in the vast, inscrutable bay, & hills

rising everywhere, a question I don't know.

PUGET SOUND

The sun here never sets. Just paler by later hour, & at dusk, or what should be dusk, fine mist of stink. The bay toothless, homeless sludgy, ferry terminal fenced off. Streets like the Tetons hem buses & taxis in the same space & thus animosity. Young women, biceps tattooed with dragons & scorpions, stare straight at you—no, into you. And your child, Quasimodo in a stroller, gawks back. We should not be this naked. Our silences our burkas: an empty stall where headless salmon rest in morning. Flower vendors rubber band arrangements. This one copper. This an explosion. Baguette unlock my mouth. I, smaller.

PENSACOLA BEACH

If my I put my ear to Daisy's   chest

I hear her grape-sized heart   pumping erratic
milliliters of blood

& she, tiny love, knows not   the unfocused, gray cloud
in the left sliver of her right
iris, a mumbling
light that will never make

sense, but nothing
ever does, not   the jigsaw of her
skin, the finger-
long bands of muscle
in her legs, her

feet, Daisy, come back   from the ocean's brink,

Daisy,   from the seagull's manic

pleading, Daisy   from my tongue
which sounds like
glass, which unfurls
down the shoreline

& the water is receding   a line of star-
fish, discarded
kelp, which Daisy

wraps around her arm
flab, & waddles   like a monster.

FROG & TOAD AREN'T FRIENDS

But gospels of the melancholy. Like too tight swimwear, their pedestrian truths corset the heart. The heart, of course, is an algae lake, an eroded bank, a barrier island with nubby peaks & scruff mesas. It's here where pines sport barbwire for needles, where tricycles rust in the rain, where no one in particular burns down pre-schools—Toad takes a branch, turns over the embers. Frog, like some great explorer, stands akimbo, nods. No one's crying. No one's snuffling. Just acres of ruinous introspection, of deep reverence for what goes wrong. Toad sighs. Toad always sighs as if his breath could collapse a thousand words. Then together they ambulate. Then together they go for a swim. Across the lake, an abandoned semi flipped on its back. Mason jars of jelly & still sheathed baguettes encircle the wreckage.

AFTER WHITMAN

Spun east on California I-10,
Terrified, exhausted, knowing what will now be,
I, a death, very young, over the ambulance, towards the yellow lines
 of eternity, the call boxes of uselessness, look no more,
Blind from the edge of my emergency lane, windshield crushed flat;
No starting eastward from Redlands, from the casinos of Indio,
From Blythe, from the south, from the border, the tourist bars, & the
 Farmacias,
From the north, from the irrigated deserts & bankrupt outlet stores,
Now having stopped, dirt where I'll soon blend,
Never to face home again, very sudden & saddened,
(But where had I called home in the first place?
And why now is it found?)

I COULD SAY

you wept hysterically while
    between thumb & forefinger, you held a scaling
        knife's semi-rusted, bent point

& pirouetted like a pirate, puncturing air
    where there should've been man, that man
        cattycorner, alternately akimbo & sipping

a flat Pabst, laughing your choked threats
    until it bored him—knife was slapped
        clear from your hand & you dangled

on some final accusation, some grand injury
    you could not birth. Snot jammed
        your sinuses like a toddler's, which I was

when I stared at the Graham crackers
    uneaten on the bread plate, booster seat
        this eruption's epicenter, I could say

you scooped & cradled me, then pushed
    me out from your arms, a rancid diaper
        neither of you knew to dispose

but you were in one chair, he in another
    as he rubbed deep circles into his temples.
        For a long time, you stared vacuously

until you pointed to my plate: I could say it was
    like chomping cardboard, a branding iron,
        a martini of glass, & I hopped down

when you were through gazing, & scrutinized
    cartoons freakishly flickering, sat so still
        the planet itself could fall like a turd,

but there are prairies regaled by wheat,
    rivers blossoming trout, & so much
        air, so many birds, & I am thankful.

Photo: Allie Hulcher

Born in the heart of Philadelphia, Pennysylvania, in 1975, JOSEPH P. WOOD is the author of four books and five chapbooks of poetry, which include *YOU.* (Etruscan Press), *Broken Cage* (Brooklyn Arts Press, finalist for the 2013 National Poetry Series), and *I & We* (CW Books, 2010). His work has appeared in venues such as *Arts & Letters Daily*, *BOMB*, *Boston Review*, *Cincinnati Review*, *Colorado Review*, *Denver Quarterly*, *Poetry London*, *Prairie Schooner*, *Verse*, among others. He is managing editor for Noemi Press and lives in Birmingham, Alabama.